Adrift

Anchoring My Grief

Copyright © 2022
All Rights Reserved

Table of Contents

Dedication	5
Acknowledgments	6
About the Author	7
When You Left	8
The Cloud	9
Adrift	10
Conversations	11
My Road	12
Yard Work	13
Warmth	15
Rainy Day	16
Signs	18
Dragonfly	20
The Wave	22
Moments	23
Green Grass	25
Before We Knew	27
Layers	29
Focus	30
But	31
The Dream	33
The Drive	35

Buttercups	37
The Storm	38
The Garden	40
Sea Glass Hunter	42
Sparkle	43
Can't Believe	45
Regret	47
Music	52
Our Grands	54
Not Yet	55
My Grief	57
Searching	58
Seasons	60
Here It Comes	62
Lessons	64
Reunion	65
Almost Two Years	67
At Odds	69

Dedication

This book is dedicated to the memory of my husband, Timothy Jackson. A legend to all that knew him.

Acknowledgments

I would like to acknowledge my family and friends for their encouragement in my writing and sharing of this very personal poetry. I only hope it will be therapeutic to others who have experienced a devastating loss.

A very special thank you to my daughter, Tori Lee Jackson, for the use of her photos.

About the Author

Debbi Sylvester Jackson is a retired Grade School Health Aide. She lives in the small town of Monmouth, Maine where she and her husband raised their four children. She began her writing journey eighteen months after the death of her husband, as a way to process her loss.

When You Left

When you left
The sunlight dimmed
The air held a chill
When you left
My heart was numb
The future uncertain
When you left
A relief remained
From holding my breath
When you left
Your pain was gone
Mine ebbed and flowed
When you left
Panic subsided
Strength slowly grew
When you left
Lessons were learned
Memories my world
When you left
Tears came and went
The sky turned to blue
When you left

The Cloud

I saw you in a cloud one day

As I was driving home

Your profile unmistakable

As white as ocean foam

Your brow and lips and beard

So very clear against the blue

A touch of gray for definition

Left no doubt that it was you

I wondered how you managed it

And timed it with precision

Your face was looking upward

As if making a decision

I thought for one brief moment

That you were here with me

The wind grew strong

The cloud broke up

It wasn't meant to be

Adrift

Take a deep breath

Go with the flow

Rise and fall with the tide

Whether fast or slow

Your anchor is lost

No rope to cast out

The shoreline so far

A rescue in doubt

As clouds start to gather

The breeze turns to wind

Drops of rain hit the bow

You feel strength from within

This storm cannot take you

To any worse fate

You've been through the worst

And unloaded your freight

The skies begin clearing

You see peeks of land

All of this time

You've had a paddle in hand

Conversations

When I talk to you

About my day

I know you hear

But cannot say

I tell you all about the house

And when the cats

Have caught a mouse

I ask advice on many chores

I hear your voice

When I'm outdoors

The kids are great

They're doing fine

I whisper

As I sip my wine

I share the news

About their sports

And chuckle at your old retorts

Sometimes it's like

You're really here

To try to wipe away

My tear

My Road

My road has taken me

To many places

I've stayed sometimes

And met new faces

I wonder

When the road is smooth

What lies ahead

What more to prove

Are there more bumps

Around the bend

I've had my share

I'm on the mend

I've done my best

To stay on track

But have been lost

When I've looked back

One thing I know

This road of mine

Will never end

There's more to find

Yard Work

The lawn needs work
It's in rough shape
Needs more than a simple rake
Twigs and branches everywhere
A utility cart is needed there
Hedges grown wild
It's been some time
Since you were here
To fight the vines
The garden littered
With leaves and weeds
A rake and a leaf blower
Is what it needs
I'm hoping that you would approve
Of my haphazard trimming
I certainly have all that I need
The tool sheds fairly brimming
The hours go by
As the yard shapes up
I think of you and smile
For you have been here
All the while

Helping me continue

Warmth

A familiar pang in my heart

As I begin my day

The years about to start

Until I push them away

You would have had

The woodstove roaring

On this crisp and chilly morn

I'll wait til I get colder

To more enjoy the warmth

This time of year

We loved so much

With many pleasures shared

Our rides to view the beauty

As our favorite music blared

The house so warm and cozy

The scent of apples filled the air

As I would cook fall comfort food

While you enjoyed the football game

It all made for the perfect mood

The house was filled with love

I miss you more than words can say

But so grateful for our life

We shared in every way

I lit the candles

You lit the fire

Rainy Day

I've always loved
A rainy day
The fish will bite
You used to say
Sometimes the sun
Just needs a break
For grass to green
And flowers wake
The gentle sound
Of a spring rain
Somehow soothes
A heart in pain
In summertime
A thundershower
Delights me so
To see such power
The pounding rain
And claps of thunder
Fill me with
A kind of wonder
A good rain
In so many ways

Helps us enjoy

The sunny days

Signs

The cardinal
Peeking in at me
While you are on my mind
The crow that showed us
Where to go
Beside the snowy pines
The songs that play
While driving
Tell me you are near
I sing with great abandon
Not holding back the tears
The cats alert me
To your presence
As they stare up at the ceiling
There's no mistaking
You are here
 Because I have that feeling
I know that you are with me
When the daffodils
First bloom
There is no pain or heavy gloom
When you show me

You are here

As long as I

Can read the signs

You've made so very clear

Dragonfly

There's no more

Perfect peace for me

Than on the water

Lake or sea

Windy day

Or calm and smooth

The kayak's gentle

Rocking moves

Transport me to

Another place

Where time is

But an empty space

To ponder life

And loss and love

To watch the eagles

High above

To hear the splash

Of jumping fish

Reminds me of

My greatest wish

To share this

Perfect peace with you

And talk of the trip

As we used to do

But now

You are the dragonfly

Who alights upon the bow

Love is forever

After all

And this will be enough

For now

The Wave

Waves of sadness

Threaten my peace

Some days I give in

It is a release

Knowing you are near

Gets me through

As grateful as I am

I still miss you

My life has changed

In many ways

Keeping so busy

I fill my days

Family friends

Laughter talks

Puttering muttering

Planning my walks

Never-ending outdoor chores

A grandchild's game

Gets me out the door

I count my blessings

When the wave comes near

It's just feeling the love

That will always be here

Moments

The cardinals chickadees
And sparrows sing
A gentle breeze
The wind chimes ring
Bees and hummingbirds
Buzzing around
Distant music
A welcome sound
As I sit outside
No screen in my lap
No blaring tv
To fill the gap
I feel a perfect peace
I'll enjoy this time
Before summer's heat
My cat's in the window
And life is sweet
These moments in time
I'm grateful for
No sadness knocking
At my door
Almost as if

I'm in a dream

Where thoughts of you

Are like a stream

That flows with ease

Over the rocks

And memories float

In a treasure box

Green Grass

The smell of fresh cut grass
Awakens memories of long ago
Of warm summer days
When Dad used to mow
The aroma of mower gas
And green clippings sprayed
After working all day
He enjoyed this task
Years later
When our yard grew scruffy
I never had to ask
Time to mow
My mate said gruffly
But he loved the job
And was happy to show
The finished landscape
And its checkered grid
I could not mistake
His obvious pride
As he sang to the music
While on his ride
Now when I push

My battery-powered machine

Through thick grass

And blacks flies

I'm only relieved

When it is done

And hope when he spies

From his heavenly view

He is proud

Of my job too

Before We Knew

The last time I kayaked

Before we knew

The water was calm

And the sky was blue

The winter had held

Constant worry

Positive thoughts

Had become blurry

When I called you

From the lake

You asked about the fish

Had I seen them jumping

As if a fervent wish

I paddled forward

In my boat

And thought about

Our constant hope

That you would be alright

I didn't know that soon

We would begin the fight

The water brought some peace

I had to take a breath

Because I did not understand

That you were close to death

Before we knew

The water was calm

And the sky was blue

Layers

Our lives are filled with layers

Of water clouds and sky

The grays and subtle grayers

Of all the books we buy

Grass soil and rocks

The rings inside a tree

Rainbows chimes of clocks

The hives of honeybees

Harmonies of music notes

The fragrance of a flower

Fabrics in a winter coat

The taste of sweet and sour

Even our emotions

Of joy and love and loss

Are like the salty ocean

From deep to waves above

There is no black and white

When it comes to our lives

But countless layers of light

And dark as we continue

to survive

Focus

Focus on the wind chime's ring

Listen to the chickadees sing

The cars racing up and down the hill

The soft breeze

The hummingbird's buzzing trill

The distant thunder

As clouds gather

All of these subtle sounds

Rather

Than your own heart

As frenzied beating starts

As your thoughts

Of sadness and pain

Threaten to sabotage

Your brain

Focus on the here and now

Sweet memories will follow

Somehow

But

I find enjoyment in watching birds

But... wait for you to call the crows

I love attending the kid's games

But..wait to hear your cheers

Walking with a friend is good

But..reach for your hand to hold

On the water is so peaceful

But... still, watch for your fish to jump

Having a drink with friends is fun

But... wait for you to crack a joke

Spending time with family

Is priceless

But... always feel an empty space

Working in the yard rewarding

But... miss your new ideas

Reading books can be relaxing

But... I miss your TV blaring

Ocean visits are my zen

But... wait for you to cast a line

Listening to music is the best

But... I hear your voice in every song

I can find joy in my life now

But... can't yet believe it's without you

The Dream

I dream of days

When we were young

Before the kids came

One by one

We only thought of summer days

And of the stars

On which we gazed

We didn't know

What life would bring

And when the winter

Turned to spring

We had no thoughts

Of future pain

When all our storms

We're only rain

We used to live for the

next day

We made our joy

Along the way

The as the years

We're coming fast

Our jobs and family

Came to pass

We knew how rich

That life could be

I'm grateful it was you and me

Who shared our love

That was the deal

And though you're gone

The dream was real

The Drive

I went for a rainy drive

And explored new roads

Our old music sound on high

Lightened up my load

You were riding with me

I could hear your voice

As you sang with great glee

The lyrics of your choice

It brought real smiles

As I drove through the rain

And quite a few miles

With no familiar pain

It means so much

Knowing you're near

Even when memories

Bring me to tears

The love we have

The family we made

Is worth the grief

That will never fade

So I'll keep going for rides

On unexplored ways

With you by my side
For the rest of my days

Buttercups

Buttercups and daisies

Dancing in the wind

Stir old childhood memories

Before real life set in

The sweet smell of clover

Overtakes my senses

Running through fields

Climbing over fences

We were young and naive

We were not aware

That in time we would grieve

The forests ours to explore

The freedom to roam

Our daily life taught us

To treasure

This world without strife

That knowledge would come

As years flew like the wind

But buttercups and daisies

Still make my heart sing

The Storm

The sky starts to darken
The breeze turning strong
I can hear the thunder
Lightening come along
The familiar excitement
Of an impending storm
Quickens my heart
But no fear is my norm
Trees begin dancing
Flashes fill the room
I close open windows
As the cats all but zoom
To hide in the closet
To wait out the din
Of torrents of rain
Pound on the roof's tin
We both so enjoyed
A good thundershower
You for the rain
And me, for the power
I can't help but think
That from heaven above

You added the thunder

You knew I would love

The Garden

Our garden was prolific
So many years ago
You tended it so carefully
To ensure the seeds you sowed
You planned the crops
That we would use
And share with others too
Your face was filled with pride
As each little seedling grew
You learned from your father
How to amend the earth
And fertilize correctly
To maximize the worth
Of produce, we would consume
The children were excited
As pumpkin flowers bloomed
While helping with the weeding
And you were fairly beaming
At the family, you were feeding
When it came to harvest time
The baskets overflowed
To waste would be a crime

So any excess you would load

And share with pleasure

Oh, the joy that filled your heart

Is a memory that I treasure

Sea Glass Hunter

She walks so slowly

With eyes on the sand

Looking for any color

That could be treasure in hand

She glimpses some blue

A small smile begins

As she picks up the glass

To feel the smooth margins

A satisfied grin

As she glances at me

To assure me no sharpness, the new giggles with glee

Her pure delight

As she finds these gifts

Fills me with love

Then she sits and sifts

Through shells and rocks

And my only thought is

As the breeze fans her blonde locks

May she always find joy

Sparkle

They only sparkle in the sunlight

I thought while picking up rocks

The beach was full of glitter

I continued my walk

And picked up special stones

So shiny in the light

But when the sun hid in clouds

My collection was not bright

I chose to bring them home

I put them in a place

That would be sure

To catch my gaze

And one by one, I held them

To admire their shine

And thought of you with love

These memories of mine

Are like this rock collection

To shine a light when sad

And when my day turns dark

And missing you feels bad

I'll bring good memories to the light

To feel the love we had

Can't Believe

Sometimes I can't believe

That you are really gone

I still think I hear your voice

When the music is on

At night I listen for your snore

And feel your weight on the bed

I dream of the days

Of the shared life we led

I think I hear the sound

Of your truck driving in

And the cats still look around

As if you are here

But I do think they see you

When your spirit is near

As I water the flowers

I hear you say deadhead

And feed them

So the blooms will amaze

That's why I can't believe

That you are really gone

So much of you is still here

And your love continues on

Regret

Do I regret any of our life
Of course, I do
But not time spent with you
I regret not listening more
When you expressed worry
I regret the busy pace
And urging you to hurry
I regret wanting my space
After a hectic day with kids
When you turned your face
For a kiss
I regret words of anger
When frustrations boiled over
Or holding a grudge
Giving a cold shoulder
I regret not saying how proud
I was of your hard work
Of keeping silent when
I saw your hurt
I hope through it all
You still felt my love
I'll never regret

Our time together
When you look down from above
Know it was forever

Music

The music transports me

To another place and time

When we were young

And your love was mine

I play the same songs

Over and over

Despite my tears

Like a four-leaf clover

I feel so lucky

We had those years

And when our children came

The melody changed

But feel I go were the same

To our family

Music is the backdrop

To all of our lives

Whether sadness or joy

We always strive

To hear the harmony

And sing the songs

With each generation

We're passing along

Our love of the music

And that love is strong

Our Grands

As I watch our granddads

Living their lives

I wish I could protect their hearts

When any pain arrives

They weathered your passing

With tears and grace

And only the next memories

And deep love in place

I'm so grateful they knew you

As long as they did

While they'll grow up without you

They'll never be rid

Of the love and guidance

You continue to give

Just know you are included

In all of our days

While we can't see you

Your sweet spirit stays

Not Yet

I look forward to reuniting

With you

But not yet

I've more sunsets to view

But don't fret

You're along for the ride

You see what I see

You're right by my side

I've more lakes to paddle

So, for now, I will stay

To spend time with loved ones

And friends along the way

I've more roads to walk

More autumns to love

But still, I can talk

To you up above

Of my everyday life

And my upcoming plans

To ride to the ocean

And walk in the sand

To snowshoe in winter

And fish with the kids

To hear the ice splinter

On bitter cold nights

To prepare for Christmas

And put up the lights

I'll see you again

When time here is done

But not yet, my love

I've more rising suns

My Grief

My grief doesn't end

It mellows and slows

There are times I embrace it

As the scent of a rose

It's familiar and sweet

It brings me close to you

My heart skips a beat

For a minute or two

My eyes blur with tears

But those moments are fewer

The sky appears bluer

Though I welcome the rain

Searching

Sometimes I wander
Around in the house
Searching for something
Not there
Quiet as a mouse
I tiptoe room to room
And feel something
Close to despair
Since you have been gone
My life without you
Goes along
But I never quite feel
That I am complete
Despite all that is real
And all that is sweet
I still yearn for your voice
Telling me, we will meet
Someday
But I do have a choice
I can live my life now
And search for the joy

That will lead me to you

Somehow

Seasons

Summer warmth brought
The flowers you tended
With such love and care
Lawn and garden thrived
While fresh veggies
Were out fare
Striper fishing was such fun
With hours in our boat
Your joy was clearly evident
When'er we were afloat
Autumn brought enjoyment
With our leaf peeping rides
You worked on getting woodpiles in
To keep us warm inside
We loved the crisp fall days
With apple picking too
And watching kids play soccer
As loud cheering would ensue
Winter was your season though
And how your eyes would gleam

While trudging on the icy lake

And breathing puffs of steam

As ice trap flags would spring

Kids squealing with excitement

You yelled bring the bait bucket

And we'll see which fish this brings

As spring arrived with yard cleanup

Your thoughts would turn

To smelting

And driving to the lakes up north

To dip nets with snow still melting

With each change of season

You found treasures they all held

You could always find a reason

To live your life so well

Here It Comes

Autumn is fast approaching
A favorite season
Is quickly encroaching
Despite August heat now
It's the very reason
That I need cool breezes
And a nip in the air
Apples getting red
A colored leaf here and there
Soccer games will soon begin
Cross Country meets have started
My daily walks will soon resume
As humid days depart
A sadness in my heart
As mid-October grows near
That was when you left
This life of ours, so dear
You did enjoy fall too
So I will celebrate
All that the season brings
And hold the memories close

And hold the memories close

As I touch our wedding rings

Here it comes

Autumn is fast approaching

Lessons

You would be so proud
Of the grandkids today
Almost two years now
They're going their own way
They are so unique
In the interests they pursue
Successes and defeats
Learning to follow through
They each have their passion
As their Grampy did
From sports to current fashion
They're each a special kid
You taught them many lessons
Although they're having fun
They didn't realize
Because they were so young
That your love and guidance
Would say with them through life

Reunion

Reconnecting with old friends
Is extra special now
Fifty years since high school
Seems so surreal somehow
We hugged and spoke
About our lives
And all that's happened since
We like to think
We are so wise
Though gray hair makes us wince
We laughed and cried at memories
And honored those not here
You would have loved
To toast a few old buddies
With a beer
Some conversations brought us back
To that special place of ours
I wouldn't trade a minute
Of those treasured hours
Fifty years is nothing
When it comes to what we feel
It's as if no time has passed

With friendships that are real

Almost Two Years

Almost two years
Since I've heard your voice
Other than old videos
Do I have a choice
Sometimes in my dreams
You make an appearance
But the bizarre themes
And scattered interference
Of my memory the next day
Leave me wanting more
Of you, I cannot have
In any other way
Almost two years
Since I've felt your hugs
Since I've heard your laugh
Missing you so much it tugs
On my heart
It seems a lifetime
We've been apart
Although I move on
And new things I will start
A part of me has been gone

Almost two years

At Odds

My time is my own

I'm free as a bird

Only me to take care of

I have the last word

I plan my days

To keep myself engaged

I'm becoming more me

In so many ways

I'm getting used to

Being the only

But you know I would trade

This new way of life

Without you here

This house can be lonely

I'm still your wife

That will never change

I wish you were here

If I could arrange

Your return to me

Together again

As it always should be

But I'll love you from here

And continue my time

To find joy each day

In this life that is mine

I Thought I Knew

I thought that my pre grief
Before you died
Gave me an edge for after
I thought for a few weeks
When I barely cried
That I knew the worst had passed
I thought I could handle
Whatever life gave
That you strength gave me a pass
Then Thanksgiving came
I was all alone
Covid had stricken the family
That first giant wave of sorrow
Hit me like a stone
My world turned upside down
There seemed no tomorrow
I felt like I would drown
But I made it through
And then I knew
That grief is never over
It comes and goes
Some days are not easy

There are real lows

But the love I feel

When I think of you

And remember why we chose

To spend our lives together

Helps soften the blue

www.ingramcontent.com/pod-product-compliance
Lightning Source LLC
Chambersburg PA
CBHW070337120526
44590CB00017B/2915